# The Forgotten Mourners

## Guidelines for Working with Bereaved Children

*Margaret Pennells and Susan C. Smith*

Jessica Kingsley Publishers
London and Bristol, Pennsylvania

First published in the United Kingdom in 1995 by
Jessica Kingsley Publishers Ltd
116 Pentonville Road
London N1 9JB, England
and
1900 Frost Road, Suite 101
Bristol, PA 19007, U S A

**Library of Congress Cataloging in Publication Data**

A CIP catalogue record for this book is available from the Library of Congress

**British Library Cataloguing in Publication Data**

A CIP catalogue record for this book is available from the British Library

ISBN 1 85302 264 0

Printed and Bound in Great Britain by
Biddles Limited, Guildford and King's Lynn

# Contents

# Introduction

We have often been asked whether children grieve. Some adults feel that children do not grieve at all; others perceive children's grief only in terms of sadness: that is, whether or not a child cries and is upset. Through our work with bereaved children we have learned that they *do* grieve, but adults often fail to recognise the presenting behaviour as that of grief. They may wish to protect children from the pain and suffering of bereavement and therefore may try to erect a protective barrier around them. It is difficult for adults to imagine that children can experience the range of emotions that adults feel at times of loss.

Similarly, when adults do recognise that children *can* have strong feelings such as anger or resentment, their reaction is often the wish to protect these children from their emotions. This denies children the means of overcoming their loss and learning to manage painful situations. Children who are bereaved live on an emotional 'see-saw' – up one moment, down the next. They have opposing attitudes to what has happened, swinging from displays of sadness to callous comments, behaviour which confuses adults and can lead them to believe that children resolve their feelings very quickly.

There are many works which highlight the significance of the making and breaking of early emotional bonds and the effect these bonds have on our psychological well-being. Studies have shown that some mental health problems presented by adults have their roots in unresolved childhood loss (Black 1978; Bowlby 1979). The process of acknowledging the event of death and expressing the related feelings of grief provides us with the opportunity for an early resolution and healthy integration of these issues. Failure to recognise and deal with these problems can lead at worst to a disturbed child, and at best to a very unhappy and unfulfilled childhood.

# CHAPTER 1

# How Children Grieve

When a bereavement occurs, children can go through the same range of emotions as adults, from feelings of shock, numbness and despair to those of anger and guilt. They may deny that the person has died by not openly showing signs of grief and continuing their life as before. They may yearn and pine for the deceased to return and long for their lost relationship. Children move through the stages of grief until they reach the stage of acceptance and are able to adjust to living without the deceased person. Although this process is much the same as the one experienced by adults, the expression of feeling is very different. Children have not developed the same conceptual skills as adults and may not easily verbalise their feelings: they show their distress through their behaviour. How children understand and react to death will therefore vary according to their age and development level.

## Age 0–2

The works of Bowlby and Erikson (Bowlby 1969, 1973, 1980; Erikson 1965) show how very young children can react to separation:

- They are able to search for the lost object and protest when the object does not appear: for example, a baby may throw a toy over the side of the pram and cry for it to be retrieved.

- At a later stage of development, the child will look over the pram for the object and may even try to retrieve it itself.

When a death occurs, the child will seek the presence of that person and experience a sense of loss, but intellectually the child will not be able to understand the permanence of that loss.

## Age 2–5

At this age the young child has developed the capacity to think, reflect, inquire and have a degree of self-control. This gives him or her a greater degree of independence and an enhanced sense of self-esteem. Experience of death at this age undermines children's self-confidence and their world becomes unreliable and insecure:

- They will cry, yearn and become clingy.

- In play they will often make attempts at reunion with the deceased person.

Intellectually they try to make sense of the events, but they will often become easily confused by explanations and will need to be told repeatedly about the loss. They will often believe that death remains reversible and so, for example, may dig up a dead animal's body to see if it has become alive again.

## Age 5–9

Having acquired the basic skills for social integration, the child finds itself in a wider social network. This may place demands on the grieving child in terms of other people's reactions, remarks from peers and so on:

- They are learning who they can trust with their thoughts and feelings.

- They will watch adults' reactions to grief and will sometimes deny their own grief in order to protect an adult's feelings.

- They have a greater awareness of guilt and may feel they were responsible for the death by illogical reasoning, such as 'Daddy died in a car accident because I was naughty the night before'.

This is also the age of fear and fantasy and a child may personalise death as a skeleton, monster, ghost or bogey man. At this age, children become curious about the rituals surrounding death and about the functions of dead bodies, often asking such questions as whether dead people need food, clothing or other things.

## Age 9–12

Greater cognitive ability at this age gives the child an awareness of the finality of death: that it is common to all living things and that it is final, universal and inevitable. This can lead the child to a recognition of the possibility of his or her own death, which is a frightening concept. In turn, this can mean:

- There is a likelihood of psychosomatic symptoms being induced.
- These symptoms may be an attempt to draw attention to the child's distress.

The child is beginning to grieve more as an adult does and may often deny feeling a sense of loss and try to 'get on with life'.

## Adolescence

Adolescents are able to grieve more as adults do, with appropriate crying, and with feelings of sadness, anger and depression. However, they may also have suicidal thoughts:

- Adolescents have powerful emotions, which may lead them to question their identity and the meaning of their life.
- They may become interested in the occult, the afterlife and the rites of different cultures.
- Socially, there may be pressure upon them to take up more adult roles, such as in the case of the death of a parent, fulfilling the role and duties of that parent.

The expectations of their peers are also important influences on the grieving process during adolescence. There may be some members of the peer group who will not know how to react when one of their group experiences a bereavement. This can lead to the bereaved young person feeling that he or she has become isolated from their group and is an emotional stranger.

## Conclusion

It must be stressed that these stages are only intended as guidelines, and children and young people may not fit neatly into these categories. It is our experience that a bereavement in childhood may advance the child's understanding of death and its consequences. It may therefore happen that a child will exhibit features described as occurring at another stage in development, regardless of his or her age.

## Key Points

- Children experience the same range of emotions as adults.
- Children are often unable to verbalise emotions and express their feelings through their behaviour.
- Children have different levels of understanding and reactions at different ages and stages of development.
- Children aged 0–2 will experience a sense of loss but will not be able to understand the permanence of that loss.
- Between the ages of 2 and 5 children will have a greater understanding of the concept of death, but will be easily confused by explanations.
- Between the ages of 5 and 9 children become more curious about death and the rituals surrounding it, and also more aware of other people's responses.
- Children aged 9–12 understand the finality of death and may become frightened by recognition of the possibility of their own death.

- Adolescents grieve more as adults, but have powerful emotions which may have a considerable effect on them.

- Children may exhibit feelings typical of a different stage of development.

# CHAPTER 2

# What Do Children Need?

## Information

Children should be told about the death in language that is clear, simple and appropriate to their age. The information needs to be given as soon as possible after the death has occurred to prevent the child hearing of it from someone else or by some other means, such as through the media. Bad news always travels fast and there will always be someone outside those immediately involved who will want to talk about what has happened. This person may not have all the facts or may have malicious intentions which makes a child very vulnerable.

When the death has been as a result of murder, suicide or multiple accident, children may have even less access to accurate information. Events seem to happen so fast that those closely involved, such as the family, are not always aware of precisely what is happening. Sometimes parents and children get separated and have to live apart for a while. This leaves children at risk of scrutiny from the press and outsiders while, at the same time, they are no longer able to rely on the security of their family network. The information children are given is not always factually correct and can be elaborated upon by the media in order to make interesting news. This could leave the child open to receiving misinformation, and they may also be vulnerable to reporters' attempts at obtaining the 'human interest' angle. The child may be interviewed and asked distressing questions, or 'pumped' for information which may leave him or her feeling confused and frightened. This can undermine the child's confidence and may complicate their grieving process as they lack a safe environment within which to explore their feelings. Not only are they trying to deal with their own shock and outrage, but may in such circumstances also be taking on board that of the general public.

## Explanations

Information given to children and young people concerning the death should be truthful and honest. If children are not told the truth they are likely to make up their own explanations in an attempt to understand what has happened. Their fantasies may often be worse than the reality, and a lack of explanation can leave children wondering whether they have caused the death because of something they said or did. Children can feel as if they are out of control when something as traumatic as a death occurs, and if they have no access to information or to sensitive help this feeling can be intensified. One way for a child to control the situation is to blame him- or herself – 'I shouted at Daddy this morning and he was angry with me and that is why his car crashed.' Situations are much easier to deal with if we have a reason for them, even if that reason has to do with something that is your own fault. Lack of explanation may lead to excessive problems with guilt in children and this can prevent them progressing through the bereavement process:

- Children's questions need to be answered as honestly as possible.

- Be prepared to admit that you don't know some of the answers rather than be tempted to make them up.

- A child can be helped to accept that not everything can be explained or understood.

If information is given sensitively and honestly, children find situations easier to deal with, whereas 'protection' from information can lead to confusion and fear.

Be aware of the language and words used to give explanations; try to avoid euphemisms at all costs. 'Granny has gone for a long sleep and will never wake up' can have a devastating effect on a child. They almost certainly will have sleep disturbances, nightmares and a fear of the dark which will take a long time to conquer. It may be easy for an adult to use the metaphor of sleep, but it is a difficult one for children to interpret, since sleep is a very large part of their life and never waking again is very difficult for them to contemplate. Similarly, the use of the words, 'passed on/over' or 'lost' can leave children confused and may cause them to believe their relative is still out there somewhere and may indeed be 'found' again. Try not to use ambiguous remarks; be clear and tell the truth, but be sensitive.

## Help with Expressing Feelings

Children learn how to grieve from the way the adults around them behave: for example, they will see whether it is acceptable to cry or not, and may ask themselves such questions as 'Is it O.K. to feel angry when I miss Daddy?'

Children have a need to be involved in the grieving process as much as possible. They should be given the opportunity to:

- view the body
- attend the funeral
- talk openly about the deceased person
- discuss their feelings for them.

If adults explain their feelings to children, children will learn what is healthy and acceptable, but if feelings are ignored children will get the message that to express them is wrong. Children may need to act out; they may behave differently, get angry or aggressive or become withdrawn and quiet in an attempt to work through their grief. If they repress their grief work, there may be a tendency for problems or feelings to be expressed inappropriately or to be misplaced. Anger is a very common emotion among bereaved children: angry and destructive behaviour shown by one boy at school was found to be rooted in his feelings towards the person who had been responsible for his brother's accidental death.

Children need help to face contradictions which can impinge on the way they grieve. Teacher might say, 'It's O.K. to feel sad and cry', and Grandma might be saying, 'Now don't cry and be a brave girl for Mummy'. How will this child know how to behave? At times children are told to 'Grow up now and take care of Mummy/Daddy', which forces them to take on a far more adult role than they are prepared for. Their behaviour often changes in these circumstances as they struggle to be a child with adult responsibilities.

Children will need help to express their feelings in safe ways which are appropriate to their age and developmental level; for example, they should be included and encouraged to help around the house, but it should not be expected of them to take on adult responsibilities.

## Reassurance

Children need reassurance that the world as they knew it has not completely disintegrated.

- A stable atmosphere provides the safety necessary for them to explore their feelings and the new environment in their family caused by the death.

- Returning to as near normal a routine as possible provides security and reliability.

Children fear for their safety and well-being and wonder, 'Who will look after me now?' particularly when it is a parent who has died. They also worry about their other parent dying and leaving them completely orphaned, or about their own death. Younger children do not have the ability to realise that death is not 'catching' and therefore unlikely to happen to everyone around them now. They may need particular reassurance that they did not cause the death, either through their actions or their thoughts. Children's imagination is a very powerful thing.

## Help with Secondary Losses

When a family member dies, not only do children have to cope with the loss of that special relationship, they often have a series of secondary losses to consider. With the death of a parent there is often a loss of income. They have to adjust to what a reduced income might mean for the family and for them as individuals, such as having fewer presents at Christmas or receiving less pocket money. This is a particularly important consideration with teenagers, who may feel they have to contribute to the family income as soon as possible by leaving school and getting a job.

Adjusting to new family situations is very difficult. Possible results of the death may be that:

- the family breaks down completely
- the children are received into care or placed in foster homes
- Mum or Dad takes a new partner – so soon after the death this may result in a child becoming very resentful that a new person has come to take the deceased parent's place so soon
- a house move becomes necessary, which may be to another village or town, thereby causing the further losses of their friends, familiar territory, school, and so on.

In the case of the death of a child the remaining siblings take on new roles: they may now become the oldest or youngest. They may lose special relationships, such as no longer having to help take care of the baby or not having an elder sibling to look up to.

Above all else, children and young people need support from everyone around them – their family, friends, school and professionals such as social workers, GPs and health visitors.

## Key Points

- Children should be told about the death in simple language.
- Children should be told promptly of the bereavement.
- Remember that children are vulnerable to the scrutiny of the press and outsiders and must be protected.
- It is important to give truthful explanations of the facts surrounding a bereavement and honest answers to children's questions
- Do not use euphemisms and try not to be ambiguous.
- Children need to be involved in the grieving process as much as possible and helped to express their feelings.
- Children may need to act out; they may become withdrawn or aggressive.
- Children need help to face contradictions in the way people speak about the death.
- Children need reassurance that their world has not disintegrated.
- Children need help to deal with secondary losses, such as loss of family income or house moves.
- Children need support from everyone around them.

# CHAPTER 3

# What Can Adults Do?

## Acknowledge Children's Grief

Some adults feel that children, if they do grieve, pass quickly through the mourning process and cope far better than adults. This can lead to comments such as: 'Sometimes I think she doesn't care her father died – she rarely cries.' However, because of their immaturity, children do not continuously evidence grief in visible ways: their periods of mourning, unlike those of adults, cannot be sustained but come in short spans.

Adults also need to be aware that children may try to protect them from their grief for fear of upsetting them at a time when perhaps things seem to be settling down. ('I didn't want to make Mummy cry again.') As we have said some children suspend their mourning process in order to take up adult roles in the family. Older children may also delay their grief if they have examinations at school or heavy home work commitments.

Children of any age are really only able to deal with one set of issues at a time, therefore multiple changes in their circumstances, such as being received into care, moving house, changing school may delay their grief.

## Understand Re-emergence of Grief

In children grief may surface – or resurface – many years later as they begin to realise the implications the death has had on their family circumstances (such as reduced finances, increased responsibility within the family, the arrival of co-habitees). If a child has not been given the full details of the death and it is only later that the whole truth emerges, the grieving process can be reactivated as the child learns to adjust to new information: for example, a child may have been told that Daddy had a heart attack, but may discover at a much later date that he committed suicide.

## Answer Questions as they Surface

Explaining death, especially to very young children, is never easy, but an appropriate beginning could be to talk about life spans, using plants, trees and animals as examples, and then to move on to human life. Obviously, the explanation that children will need should correspond to their age and developmental level:

- Simple, honest and straightforward answers are the most helpful, as children do need to be told the truth.
- They do not, however, need to know everything in one go.

- Predict some questions that may be asked and have some answers ready.
- It is advisable to find out what the child has been told already.
- If the information giver is not a member of the family, he or she must be sure to check any specific religious beliefs or feelings about death and afterlife before speaking to the child.

If a child receives veiled comments and half-truths, these can create fears and fantasies in the imagination which may be worse than the reality of the situation; for example, children need to know what a cremation is. One child we worked with was told that Mummy was in the small casket which contained the ashes. She imagined that Mummy's body had shrunk and was a miniature doll-like figure, because the process of cremation had not been explained to her. We must use language that is clear and logical when giving explanations, and should not invent stories to soften the impact. Another child was told that Daddy was above the clouds, driving his bus. Naturally, this led the child to have many concerns and questions about buses being above the clouds; his first trip in an aeroplane will soon show him the truth of the situation.

## Anticipate Behaviour Problems in Bereaved Children

Because children's worries and fears are expressed through their behaviour, a death in the family could activate the question 'Who's next?' and cause anxiety, which children may then act out. Adults need to understand and normalise this behaviour by disciplining children as normal. However, a balance needs to be struck, and sensitivity to the child's anxiety is the key. This can sometimes be difficult if adults are caught up with their own grieving and do not have the time or energy to cope with demanding children. It can happen that the usual house rules and limitations lapse, which may exacerbate the child's difficult behaviour, since the child senses that the 'norm' no longer applies: this adds to the feelings of insecurity that he or she is experiencing.

Children, likewise, will feel angry, frustrated, worried and upset, and will need help to express these feelings in safe and appropriate ways (see Chapter 2, pp.18–19).

## Include Children in the Mourning Process

Adults naturally wish to protect children from the pain and suffering that a bereavement brings and may thus want to exclude them from the rituals of mourning.

- Exclusion can affect children, making them feel angry at being left out, ignored and disregarded.

- Their grief can be complicated and delayed as they are not sure what has happened to the dead person, and have not had a chance to say goodbye.

- Children should therefore be involved in the rituals as much as possible and given a choice in such matters as whether or not to go to the funeral, or to view the body.

- Adults need to explain to the child what is to happen and what it will be like, and then on the information received the child can make a choice.

- Very few children will exclude themselves.

The funeral can be a traumatic time for families, where the adults are completely occupied with their own grief. If children *are* to attend the funeral, try to ensure that an adult who is known to them, but is not part of the immediate family, will take special responsibility for them during the ceremony and will be ready to explain things to the child and answer any questions that may arise. Sometimes families like to include children in other bereavement rituals, such as discussing with them the headstone to be placed on the grave or the plaque in the crematorium and what is to be written on it.

## Keep the Memory of the Person Alive

A small child's ability to remember the deceased will be limited and inadequate, and therefore assistance with remembering the person may be necessary up to adolescence. Mementos of the deceased person are important, so try to set aside something that the child can keep. As children worry that they may forget what the person looked like, it is helpful to keep a photograph or to prepare an album which may aid the child's remembrance. When families are separated and split, obtaining mementos from the other party can be difficult, but a photograph alone may be sufficient to help a child with recall and to aid resolution.

Special times, like anniversaries, birthdays and Christmas, need to be acknowledged. Children will remember the anniversary of the death and the birthday of the deceased and will need to share their thoughts and feelings on these days, or to mark them in some special way, such as taking flowers to the cemetery, lighting a candle or making a card.

On the child's birthday or at Christmas, remember that the child will be missing the card and present usually given by the deceased, and may say 'I left a space on the mantelpiece where I usually put the birthday card I get from by brother,' or 'There was no Daddy to give me a Christmas present this year.'

> REMEMBER: Even if relationships have been difficult, it is important to keep the memory of the deceased alive; never pretend that they never existed.

## Be Gentle with Yourselves

The process of grieving can be long, hard and painful. There are many things to be done, adjustments to be made and situations to come to terms with. It is difficult to cope with a child when one can barely cope with oneself, so try not to cope on your own. Involve other people, such as relatives or a teacher, in giving support to the child. Sometimes children – like adults – will find it easier to talk to someone from outside the family environment: try not to see this as a failure, but simply as the child's perfectly natural need to express his or her thoughts and feelings to someone who is less emotionally involved.

If you can, take time to relax and spoil yourself – and try not to feel guilty about this. Do something you enjoy, such as a soak in the bath, a walk in the country, reading, or a more physical pursuit which may help to release pent-up feelings.

**Key Points**

- Adults must acknowledge children's grief.
- Children often do not show their grief in visible ways; their periods of mourning come in short spans.
- Children may try to protect adults from their grief.
- Children may suspend their mourning process; older children may delay it.
- Multiple changes in their circumstances may delay children's grief at any age.
- Grief may resurface very much later, especially if children have not been given all the facts at the time.
- Explain death as simply as possible, in manageable steps that they are able to take in.
- Treat children as normal as much as possible, but expect possible behavioural problems.
- Include children in the mourning process and allow them to choose which rituals they wish to be included in.
- If children attend the funeral, explain what is happening.
- Keep the memory of the person alive, especially at anniversaries.
- Remember the needs of the adults involved too.

# CHAPTER 4

# What Can Schools and Teachers Do?

## Look Out for Changes in Behaviour

Schools and teachers have a significant role to play in the life of the bereaved child. Some children see school as a haven of peace and normality in contrast to the trauma and upset at home. They may therefore act as if the bereavement has not occurred in an attempt to at least preserve one area of their life as 'normal'. Conversely, other children may find school is the place to express their feelings, so always be alert to changes in the child's behaviour: whether the child becomes more withdrawn or more aggressive, for example.

- Some children may be more vulnerable and anything will trigger tears, some may exhibit mood swings, and others may present with psychosomatic symptoms (headaches, stomach aches, general 'not well' feelings).

- Depression is more evident in older children.
- Adolescents may have suicidal thoughts, and some make suicide attempts.

Adolescence is a particularly difficult time and a bereavement at this stage makes it even more so: it may not always be easy to distinguish behaviour which might be rooted in the young person's reaction to the bereavement from normal adolescent behaviour. Adolescents can more fully appreciate the implications of death for the family, and are struggling with their own ideas about issues of life and life after death.

It is important to remember that all children will act differently and it could be months or even years before they show the impact that the death has had on them. It is therefore often difficult for teachers to relate current behaviour to a bereavement that occurred many years ago. Problems related specifically to school may emerge, such as falling behind with school work or a lack of concentration. Other children may react in quite the opposite manner by overworking and putting all their energies into school activities, in order to avoid the pain of grief.

### Be Aware of Potential School Refusal

Bereaved children sometimes feel they cannot face school at all. They are not sure who knows in school, which teachers or pupils have been told about the bereavement. They may be unsure of what reaction they will get when they turn up for school, so do try to ensure that all members of staff concerned with the child know about the bereavement, so that the child is not inadvertently hurt by some chance remark. The child's peers react differently and they are often not sure of how to approach the bereaved child. They may ignore the child and not mention the death, or they may overwhelm the child with so many questions that he or she cannot cope. Bereaved children often find they are taunted because they are now 'different', and hurtful remarks such as 'I'm glad your Mum has died' or 'It's the best thing that ever happened to your family' can lead to increased aggression or to the child failing to come to school. Bereaved children also worry that others may die and can be especially afraid to leave home in case something else happens there.

## Create a Supportive Atmosphere

Teachers can help a child by creating a supportive atmosphere whereby the bereaved child feels they can talk and share their story and their feelings:

- Allow the child to cry or be angry, and encourage expression of feelings.

- Bereavement is also a learning experience for the rest of the class: it can help them to understand that grief is normal and natural.

- Bereavement can widen a class's knowledge of the grieving and mourning processes for other cultures and religions.

Be aware, however, that there may be times when the bereaved children need to go to a quiet place with someone if they are very upset. Generally, it is best to expect them to function as normally as possible. Try not to separate them from the rest of their peer group: bereaved children fear they have become 'abnormal', and separation or special treatment will only serve to increase this fear. They are asking questions such as 'Who am I now?' and 'Are we still a family?' and therefore need plenty of reassurance that they are still 'normal' and not 'different'.

It does the child no good at all to point out how grateful they should be, that they still have a mum, brother or sister. No one can ever replace the person who has died. It is also very unhelpful to make such comments as, 'I thought you would feel better by now.' Remember that children will grieve at their own pace and in their own time.

It is a very good idea to try to ensure that the class or school library has some appropriate books on loss and death for the bereaved and other children to read. Such books can include the rites and rituals of other cultures and ethnic groups, so loss and death can be seen as a universal occurrence with a variety of responses. If there are several bereaved children, it may be helpful to create a network whereby they can link up with one another in the school, so that they need not feel so isolated and alone in their situation.

## Acknowledge the Death

The class teacher at the school can create a means for acknowledging the death by having some kind of memorial. The memorial could be a special school assembly involving the whole school, or a small simple service in the classroom which, for example, could involve drawings and lighted candles.

- Some schools have a memorial book into which the names of any deceased known to the children are put.

- If the deceased person is known to the whole school, such as in the case of the death of a member of staff or pupil, then some memorial like a clock, plaque or piece of equipment can be bought as a significant reminder of the deceased person.

It is also important to remember anniversaries, such as Mothering Sunday or Father's Day, and to be aware that there may be children on these days who do not have a mother or a father. Children have reported going off to the toilets to cry or not going to school at all if they know that discussion of such topics is planned.

### Create Links with Home

Contact with the bereaved child's family can be useful in helping to understand the child in school, as the family pattern of grieving will have its effect on the child. As we mentioned in Chapter 2, children learn how to grieve from the adults around them. The family may take the 'stiff upper lip' attitude and not outwardly express its grief – the child may therefore follow this mode of coping; other families may be overwhelmed by grief, and the child feels 'lost' as all normal patterns of living are disrupted: they may have many tearful periods and feel that they will never recover from what has happened.

If it is a child in the family who has died, the family may idolise that child's memory. This can cause problems for the bereaved child, in cases where the dead sibling becomes a powerful ghost that the parents cannot let go of in favour of the living child. The child may therefore feel it has to live up to the expectations the parents had of the deceased sibling, and this can cause anger, jealousy and resentment. If the parents are stuck in this mode of grieving, be aware that the bereaved child's needs may be ignored and he or she may encounter difficulties in resolving his or her own grief.

Some bereaved families have already been divided by divorce and separation. The child may not only be coping with the bereavement but with many other changes in the home resulting from it. A death in this family could lead to the child going to live with their other parent, being fostered or even adopted, or they may have to cope with their remaining parent's new partner.

> REMEMBER to always be aware that some children, especially those who have had a difficult relationship with the deceased, or who have been abused by them, may in fact be relieved and happy that the death has occurred and therefore may not grieve in the expected way.

## Create a School Policy

The creation of a school policy can cover such issues as whom to tell, where the child can go when upset, and which teachers will be identified to support a child. The school should consider how to create a memorial and what local resources are available to support bereaved families. The issue of staff training should also be addressed, and consultation should be made with other professionals when necessary.

Loss and death could be included as a subject in the curriculum so that these events are seen as a natural – if difficult – part of life.

## Key Points

- Schools and teachers have a significant role to play.

- Be aware of changes in behaviour and of different ways that children may express their grief.

- All children will act differently, and it may be a considerable time before they show the impact of the death.

- Be aware of the responses of the child's peers, which may lead to school refusal.

- Create a supportive atmosphere in which the child can talk and share feelings.

- Be aware of the child's need for privacy, but do not separate them from their peer group.

- Try to ensure that the school has a library of appropriate books.

- Acknowledge the death by some sort of memorial in the school, and remember anniversaries.

- Create links with home.

- Remember that in some cases children may be relieved by the death and may not grieve in the expected way.

- Ensure that there is a school policy.

# CHAPTER 5

# What Can Social Workers Do?

## Support the Bereaved Child

A bereavement in the family, especially the death of a parent, may mean many changes for the children involved. Social workers may be asked to look for alternative care arrangements or foster placements or to assist with moving a child from the custody of one parent to that of the other. It needs to be recognised that if other major changes occur as a result of the bereavement, the child needs time to adjust to his or her new situation before being able to begin the grieving process.

Social workers can:

- help children understand the impact of bereavement on their family and why the family may be functioning differently

- explain the different ways in which people react to a bereavement

- provide some space and time for individual work with children, allowing them to tell their story and express their feelings

- be alert to the child's reaction to a bereavement and help parents, teachers and other adults to understand that possible emotional and behavioural problems in the child may be linked to the child's grieving process.

Social workers may be role models for other adults when talking to the children (in such matters as how to approach the subject of death, or what words to use).

### Help and Support the Bereaved Family

After a death in the family there are often many practical arrangements to be made. As the family is often still very shocked and numb, someone known to them, but outside the family circle, can provide the information, guidance and support needed at this time.

As social workers may become involved soon after the bereavement has occurred, they can be useful in helping the family to face the reality of the bereavement and preventing denial occurring. Social workers need to be alert to the family's grieving patterns and recognise when a family – or member of it – is 'stuck' in the grieving process and needs help to move on.

- Some families may keep a room as a perpetual shrine to the dead person; although this may be a normal initial reaction to the bereavement, the family would need help if it were still operating at this level many years later.

· Families can also become obsessive about visiting the grave long after the person has died, and children can be caught up in this process and need freeing from it, as their own pattern of grieving may be quite different.

Social workers can play an important role in helping families who have become caught in such behaviour patterns.

Social workers can also be alert to the family giving their children some form of overcompensation after a bereavement, usually in an effort to make up for the loss, or to help to lessen the resultant pain of it. Some families may fear something may happen to the surviving children and therefore become over-protective of them. In other cases, the opposite can also happen, whereby the surviving children are rejected as the parents idolise the dead child and withdraw from their living children. In such instances, social workers can help the family to look at their grief reactions, must be alert to guilt, anger and rejection and can encourage the expression of feelings within the family.

A bereavement in the family will sometimes highlight existing family problems, and communication between its members may be especially difficult, since they are all grieving in their own way and showing it at different times. The child will need help to understand this.

The family – or individuals within it – may also need specialist help. Social workers can help the family to seek and make use of bereavement counselling services where this is appropriate.

## Key Points

- Social workers can support the child and help them understand bereavement and its impact on them and their family.

- Social workers can be role models for other adults in how to talk to children about death and bereavement.

- Social workers can help the family face the reality of the bereavement and help them through the process.

- Social workers should be alert to the family treating the child in a different way – either over-compensating, or rejecting.

- The family may need specialist help.

CHAPTER 6

# Working With Bereaved Children

## Family Work

This has usually been the preferred method of working with the bereaved, since grief affects everyone in the family to a greater or lesser degree. A death can change the dynamics of the family by creating new roles and undermining accepted patterns of behaviour. Each family member will grieve at a different pace, and this may sometimes create conflict and misunderstanding. For example, a man may contain his expression of grief and withdraw, while his wife may be more expressive and, therefore, feel either unsupported by him or fail to recognise his grief.

Family work aims to:

- address the way the family functions

- create understanding
- help family members to progress through the stages of grief.

This method is particularly helpful for addressing those issues that arise when a family is stuck at a particular stage of grief, such as still keeping a room as a shrine after a protracted period. People working with families may also need to help family members understand that their child's behaviour could be a manifestation of that child's grief. A family worker may help them understand what children experience at different stages of development.

Family sessions can be used as a forum to discuss practical issues following a bereavement (such questions as how frequently they need to visit the grave and how to include children in the mourning process). It is often useful to have a facilitator to help a family discuss these difficult topics and to ensure that the needs of each member of the family are met. Families may also need help in understanding the source of their present pattern of functioning. Family therapy may help each member to examine their own history of loss and their coping methods.

## Individual Work with Children

Family work is undoubtedly of great value, but individual work with children also has a significant role to play. Whilst the adult members of the family may move on in their grief, a child may remain stuck at a particular stage and therefore require some individual work. This gives the child an opportunity to work through grief at his or her own level of understanding by using tools and methods which correspond to the child's age and developmental level; for example, play and painting can be used in situations where it is difficult for a child to verbalise emotions.

The child sometimes needs to be given space and time away from the family to express very deep feelings which he or she believes may upset or confuse the adults. Children are also very curious and often want to ask questions which may shock adult members, such as what happens to a dead body. Working on an individual level with children also provides the forum for them to express fears and fantasies, clear up confusion and come to terms with changes within the family.

## Group Work with Children

Whilst family work and individual counselling are valid means of helping bereaved children, we feel that these methods do not address specifically a child's isolation in grief or give them peer group support. The main aim of group work is to create a space for children to share with peers, thereby fostering a sense of mutual identity which helps to stabilise relationships outside the group.

Goals that can be achieved by using group work are:

- an alleviation of isolation
- an increase in self-esteem
- the giving of reassurance and support
- reducing a child's feelings of being powerless and stigmatised.

A bereavement group offers children the chance to 'normalise' their situation, to mix with others who have had similar experiences so that they feel less isolated and 'different', and to provide a mutual aid system, by sharing with others and allowing an opportunity to hear possible solutions and ideas.

When using group work as your chosen method of working with bereaved children, you should attempt to achieve the following goals:

1.  Help them to express the effect the loss has had (expression of feelings).

2.  Increase their sense of the reality of the loss.

3.  Provide an opportunity for them to voice fears and concerns.

4.  Create opportunities for them to acquire knowledge.

5.  Encourage a healthy withdrawal from the deceased.

6.  Help them to readjust after the loss – to seek new relationships, to adapt to a new position or role within the family or to become accustomed to a substitute family.

### Planning a Bereavement Group

Consideration should be given to the source of referrals, the content of the programme and the number of sessions. The venue for sessions and provision of transport are also important issues, and enough space and time have to be provided to enable the group to run as smoothly as possible. Equipment and materials – books, paper, paints – should be obtained in advance.

It is advisable to keep children in age-appropriate groups as they will be at similar developmental stages.

We suggest the following groupings:

6–8 years

9–12 years

12 plus.

The sessions should include drink and biscuits to help children settle and to provide a symbol of 'sharing'. The content of each session should be as varied as possible to avoid boredom. However, do not 'overfill' the session as this will result in tasks remaining uncompleted. Use work techniques the children are familiar with, such as play, painting, working with clay, dressing-up or acting. Some time for free activity should be built into the session to allow children to 'let off steam'.

REMEMBER that even teenagers like to let off steam and may want to regress to simple contact games in order to achieve this.

The aim of the group should be to help the children come to terms with their bereavement. In order to facilitate this you should explore the stages of grief and mourning:

- shock, numbness, disbelief
- anger, guilt, denial
- yearning, searching
- acceptance

Plan the group's ending as soon as possible: this makes the children realise there will be another ending in their life soon but it will be planned and they will be part of it. Have a party, perhaps, or go out for a meal, or use the available local amenities (skating, swimming).

## Key Points

- Family work is useful since the whole family is affected.

- Each family member will grieve at a different pace; family work may help members understand one another

- Family sessions can be used to discuss practical issues.

- Individual work with children will allow them to work through their grief at their own level.

- Group work with children allows them to share with peers, thereby fostering a sense of mutual identity and of self-esteem.

- Careful consideration should be given to practical issues when planning a bereavement group.

- Some time for free activity should be built into the session.

- It is helpful to explore the stages of grief and plan the group's ending early.

CHAPTER 7

# Guidelines for Effective Coping

It is important for any adult working with bereaved children to recognise the effects of such work on him- or herself. Being the receptor for many strong emotions can be damaging and stressful. The need to 'counsel the counsellors' has recently been highlighted by professionals involved in counselling children and their families in the wake of such disasters as the Bradford fire, the sinking of the *Herald of Free Enterprise*, or the Hillsborough Football Stadium disaster. The many workers (carers, counsellors) involved in such traumatic events themselves have a need to offload their feelings and receive support. This is also true for any adult faced with a bereaved child who is experiencing and sharing distress. No matter how effective our interventions and efforts are in helping the child, we are witnesses to that child's suffering, and this can leave us feeling helpless and powerless.

We soon recognise that we are unable to stop the pain of bereavement or prevent the feelings of guilt experienced by the bereaved person. Sometimes, too, there is the risk of becoming overinvolved, and the boundaries between the caregiver and the bereaved person become blurred. We can find ourselves doing too much, giving too much of our time to one situation and becoming overwhelmed.

People working in community institutions, such as schools and residential homes, also have particular problems to face, since their counselling can involve large numbers of children, all affected by one event, such as the death of a pupil, the tragic killing of children in class by a gunman, or the well-publicised event in which children were killed and maimed by a man bursting into their school with a flamethrower. Not only are there the immediate pupils to deal with, but staff, parents, the community as a whole, and – importantly – the media. One event can overwhelm the lives of many.

It is to be hoped that the many professionals who are working constantly with death and dying (such as those in the hospice movement) will have recognised the need for protective measures and effective support systems to help them cope. Staff whose needs are met, contained and – one hopes – relieved, will be able to invest further energy in their work. A lack of supportive structures will often lead to staff experiencing 'burn-out' or suffering breakdowns, can increase the level of absenteeism from work through illness, and will frequently result in constant staff changes.

Professionals working in the field of bereavement therefore need:

- a healthy management structure
- consultation
- staff meetings
- key workers
- regular supervision
- effective communication
- clear policies
- clear definition of roles
- clear boundaries
- recognition of personal boundaries as a caregiver/counsellor
- recognition of the limitations of efforts and interventions

Any parent or adult when faced with bereaved children will need to acknowledge his or her own personal limitations. There is only so much we can do. It will therefore often be helpful to:

- know other people who are willing to share the task, such as friends or relatives
- be familiar with the resources offered by the community (counselling services such as CRUSE, Compassionate Friends)
- recognise when to refer the case to another caregiver for more professional help – this is vital.

Some children may need to be referred for further professional help if they show evidence of:

1.  persistent anxieties about their own death

2.  destructive outbursts

3.  compulsive caregiving

4.  euphoria

5.  accident-proneness

6.  unwillingness to speak about the deceased person

7.  expression of only positive or only negative feelings about the deceased person

8.  inability or unwillingness to form new relationships

9.  daydreaming – resulting in poor academic performance

10. stealing

11. school phobia

As we said earlier in the book, caregivers need to be gentle with themselves. Time spent away from the bereaved child is as important as time spent with them. Learning to relax, to switch off, to invest our energy in something else – sports or hobbies – helps with the management of stress and thus helps us to become more effective helpers when the situation demands it.

Working with bereaved children is challenging. It is not all stress and strain; there can be times of laughter and fun as well as times of sadness and grief.

This guide is intended to encourage carers to take up the task of helping these children – we all have gifts, skills and talents that can be used, and a listening attitude can be as effective as the most profound piece of therapy. We all have a part to play.

## Key Points

- It is important for adults to recognise the effects of grief work with children on themselves.
- Such work can make professionals feel helpless and powerless.
- There is a risk of boundaries becoming blurred.
- Effective support systems are necessary.
- It is important for adults working with bereaved children to recognise their own limitations.
- Some children may need to be referred for further professional help.
- Working with bereaved children is challenging; it is important that caregivers give themselves time to relax and 'switch off'.
- We all have a part to play with bereaved children.

# References

Black, D. (1978) The bereaved child. *Journal of Child Psychology and Psychiatry 19*, 287–292.

Bowlby, J. (1969) *Attachment and Loss*, volume 1. London: Hogarth Press.

Bowlby, J. (1973) *Attachment and Loss*, volume 2. London: Hogarth Press.

Bowlby, J. (1979) *The Making and Breaking of Affectional Bonds*. London: Tavistock.

Bowlby, J. (1980) *Attachment and Loss*, volume 3. London: Hogarth Press.

Erikson, E. (1965) *Childhood and Society*. Harmondsworth: Penguin Books.

# Resources

**Book List**

*For reading with children*

Althea (1982) *When Uncle Bob Died.* London: Dinosaur
  Publications.
  For 5–8-year-olds. Talks about expressing anger, fear, memo-
  ries and sadness.

Mellonie, Brian and Ingpen, Robert (1983) *Beginnings and
  Endings with Lifetimes in Between.* Limpsfield, Surrey: Dragons
  World Books.
  For 5–8-year-olds. Simple explanation of lifespans for every
  living thing.

Sims, Alicia (1986) *Am I Still A Sister?* Slidell, LA: Big A and Co.
Suitable for use with 8–10-year-olds. Written by a young person following the death of her baby brother. Covers a wide range of situations and emotions.

Stickney, Doris (1984) *Waterbugs and Dragonflies*. London: Mowbray.
Suitable for use with 5–8-year-olds. Simple explanation of death and how a return to life is not possible; uses the metaphor of insects.

Varley, Susan (1985) *Badger's Parting Gifts*. London: Collins (Lions).
Good for 5–10-year-olds. Focus is on remembering in positive ways.

## Books for teenagers

Department of Social Work, St. Christopher's Hospice (1989) *Someone Special Has Died*. London: St. Christopher's Hospice.
For age 12 and over. Covers a range of emotions and situations. Available from St. Christopher's Hospice, 51–59 Lawrie Park Road, London SE22 6DZ.

Hospice of St. Francis (1990) *Young People and Bereavement*. Berkhamstead: Hospice of St. Francis.
For age 12 and over. Gives useful contact addresses. Available from Hospice of St Francis, 27 Shrubland Road, Berkhamstead, Hertfordshire HP4 3HX.

Lloyd, Carole *The Charles Barber Treatment*. London: Walker Books.
Age 14 and over. Story of a boy whose mother dies suddenly; covers a range of emotions and shows how life can continue.

Mystrom, Carolyn (1990) *Emma Says Goodbye*. Oxford: Lion Books.
For age 12 and over. Recalls a special relationship with an aunt and the problems of a long illness.

Wallbank, S. (1991) *Facing Grief: Bereavement and the Young Adult*. Cambridge: Lutterworth Press.

Williams, Guinevere and Ross, Julia (1983) *When People Die*. Edinburgh: Macdonald.
Age 14 and over. Explains in detail how a body dies and deals with practical issues.

## Books for Professionals

Dyregov, Atle (1991) *Grief in Children*. London: Jessica Kingsley Publishers.

Grollman, E.A. (ed) (1969) *Explaining Death to Children*. Boston, MA: Beacon Press.

Heegaard, M.E. (1988) *When Someone Very Special Dies*. Minneapolis, MN: Woodland Press.
For use with 5–10-year-olds. Workbook and facilitator's guide. Pages for drawing free expression of feelings.

Rando, Therese A. (1984) *Grief, Death and Dying*. Champaign, IL: Research Press Co.
Good general text book, not overcomplicated for the beginner. Chapter 2 explains grief reactions to loss and task necessary to aid readjustments.

Smith, Susan C. and Pennells, Margaret (1993) 'Bereaved children and adolescents'. In Kedar Nath Dwivedi (ed) *Group Work with Children and Adolescents*. London: Jessica Kingsley Publishers.

Staudacher, Carol (1988) *Beyond Grief*. Souvenir Press.
A guide for recovering from the death of a loved one.

Worden, J. W. (1983) *Grief Counselling and Grief Therapy*. Tavistock Publications.
Good general textbook. Easy to understand.

Ward, Barbara and Associates (1993) *Good Grief 1: Exploring Feelings, Loss and Death with Under Elevens*. London: Jessica Kingsley Publishers.

Ward, Barbara and Associates (1993) *Good Grief 2: Exploring Feelings, Loss and Death with Over Elevens*. London: Jessica Kingsley Publishers.
Book one – age under 11; book two – age 11 and over. Good resources for teachers.

Wells, Rosemary (1988) *Helping Children Cope with Grief*. London: Sheldon Press.

**Videos**

1. That Morning I Went to School.

2. Childhood Grief.

Both videos can be bought or hired from Sister Margaret Pennells, Child & Family Consultation Service, 8 Notre Dame Mews, Northampton NN1 2BG. Telephone (0604) 604608.